My First ARCTIC

Nature Activity Book

Nature North of the 60th Parallel

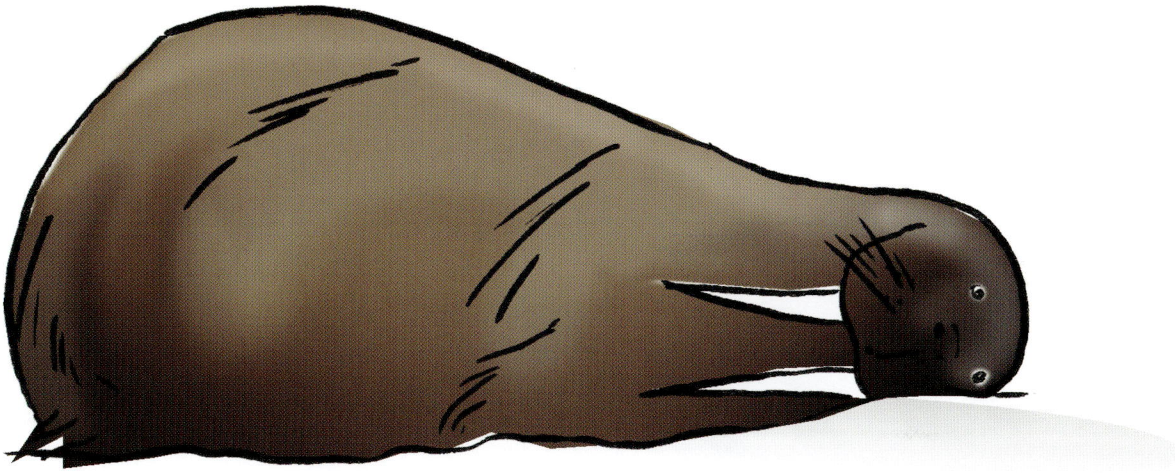

James Kavanagh
Illustrations by Raymond Leung
and Steve Patton

Printed in China. For further information, contact Waterford Press Inc., 428 N. 24th Street, Phoenix, AZ 85008.
To order, call 800-434-2555; Fax: 602-681-3343. To share comments, email us at editor@waterfordpress.com
For information on custom-published products, call 800-434-2555.
ISBN: 978-158355-586-6

WORD SEARCH

Arctic Mammals

ARCTIC FOX

P	O	L	A	R	B	E	A	R	U
O	W	A	W	D	K	G	R	Y	Q
Z	O	R	O	D	V	R	C	Y	V
D	L	T	O	L	D	I	T	G	T
W	V	W	I	B	W	Z	I	T	U
Y	E	H	S	H	R	Z	C	T	N
G	R	A	Y	W	O	L	F	U	P
A	I	E	R	P	V	Y	O	V	K
X	N	V	P	Z	Y	Z	X	J	R
T	E	F	A	S	Z	L	U	Q	N

GRIZZLY

POLAR BEAR

WOLVERINE

GRAY WOLF

answers

WHO AM I?

Draw a line between the Arctic animal and its name.

1. 

2. 

3. 

4. 

King Crab

Caribou

Snowy Owl

Walrus

answers

1. Walrus
2. Snowy Owl
3. King Crab
4. Caribou

CONNECT THE DOTS

I am a large hoofed mammal with curving horns. My soft wool keeps me very warm during the long winter.

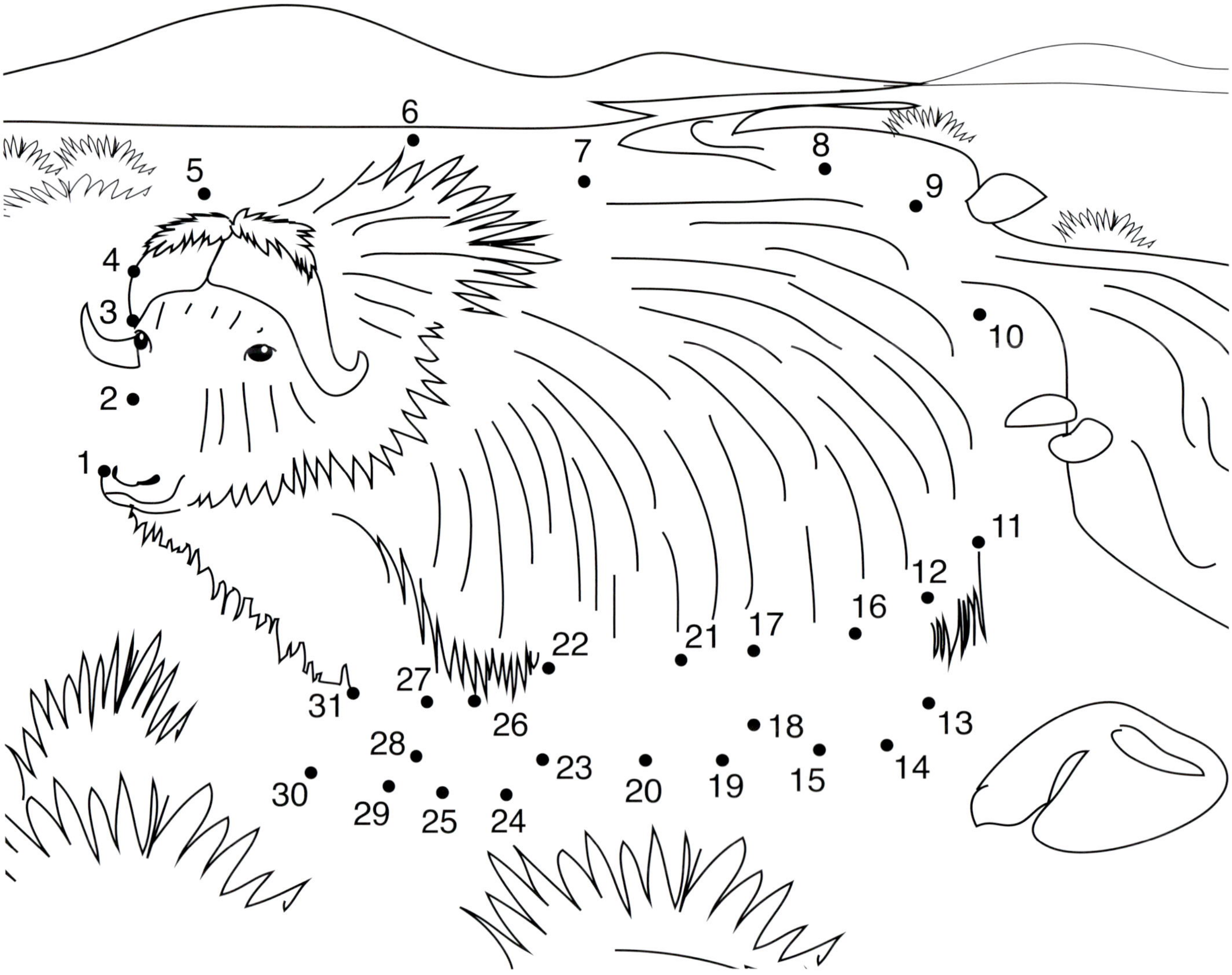

Who am I?

answer
Musk Ox

SHADOW KNOW-HOW

Can you identify these arctic animals?

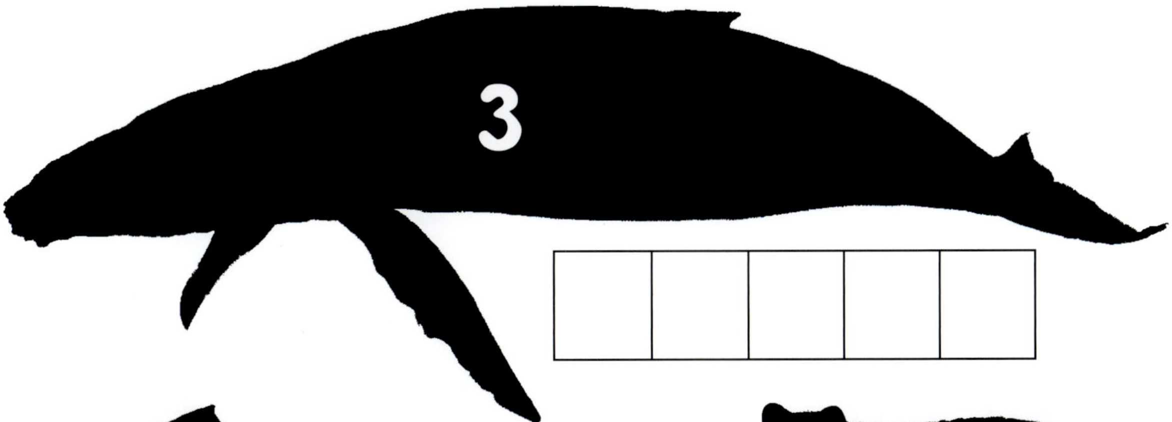

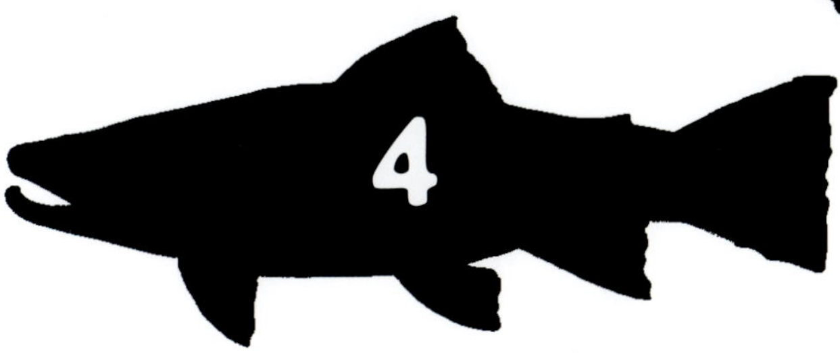

answers

1. Bear
2. Rabbit
3. Whale
4. Fish (salmon)
5. Fox

ORIGAMI

Starting with a square piece of paper, follow the folding instructions below to create this fox.

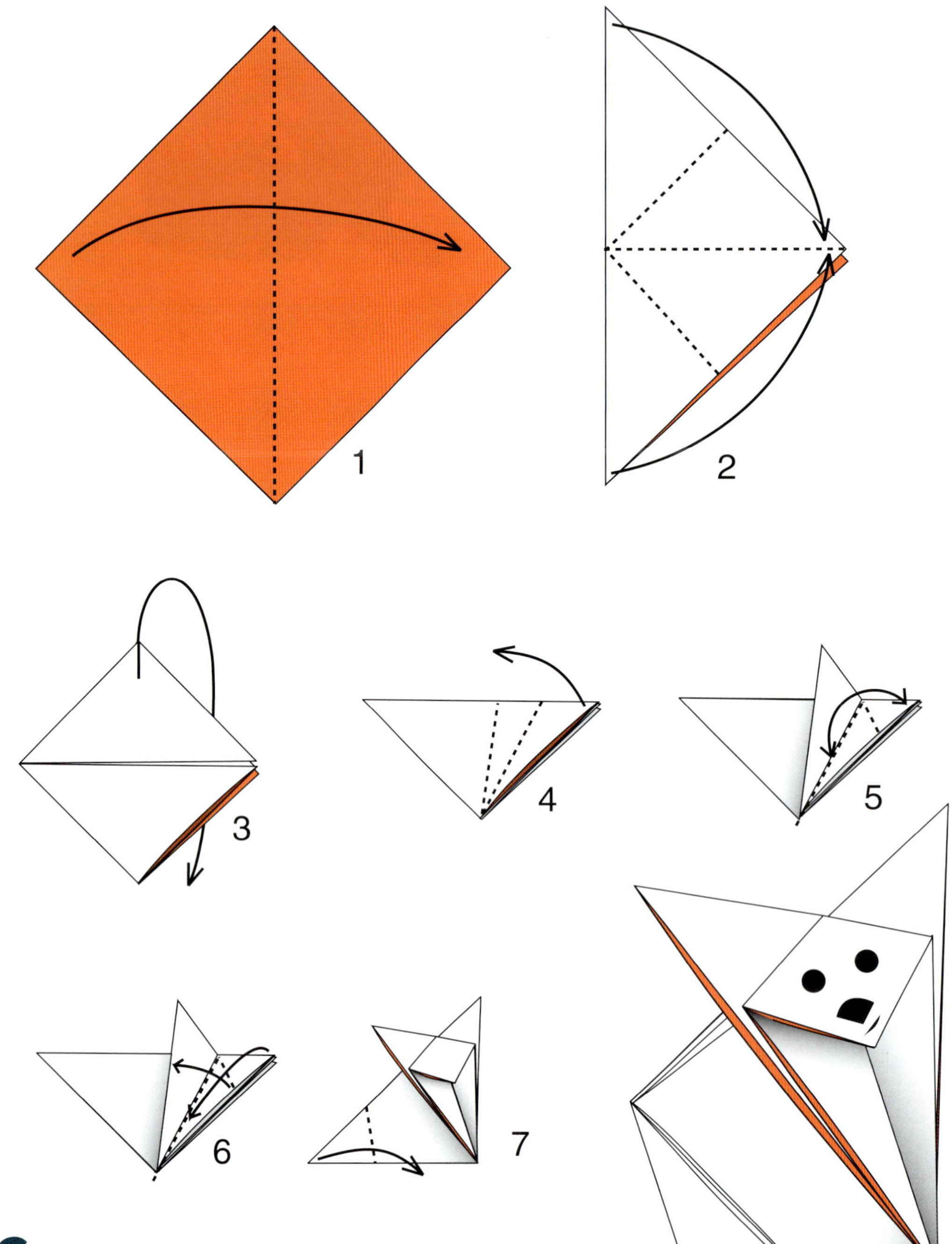

Draw on its eyes, nose and mouth.

MAKE WORDS

The **polar bear** is a clever hunter. When sneaking up on prey, it will sometimes cover its black nose so it can't be seen in the snow.

How many words can you make from the letters in its name?

______________________ ______________________

______________________ ______________________

______________________ ______________________

______________________ ______________________

______________________ ______________________

answers

Possible answers include: Alp, arab, bar, bare, barrel, boa, boar, bore, ear, lab, labor, lap, lob, oar, pale, par, parlor, parole, peal, pear, pearl, pole, real, reap, rear, rebar, roar, rob, robe, role, rope

WHO AM I?

Draw a line between the animal and its name.

1. 

2. 

3. 

4. 

Eider Duck

Flying Squirrel

Killer Whale

Pink Salmon

answers

1. Flying Squirrel
2. Pink Salmon
3. Eider Duck
4. Killer Whale

Be an Artist

Draw this walrus by copying it one square at a time.

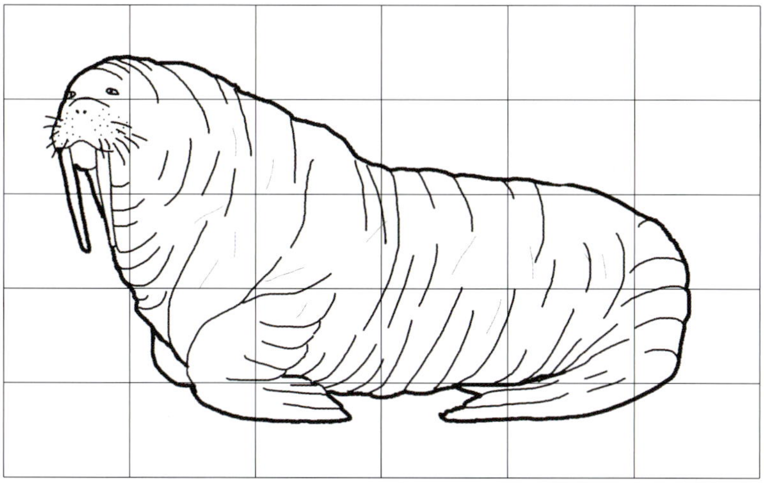

WORD SEARCH

Arctic Seashore Animals

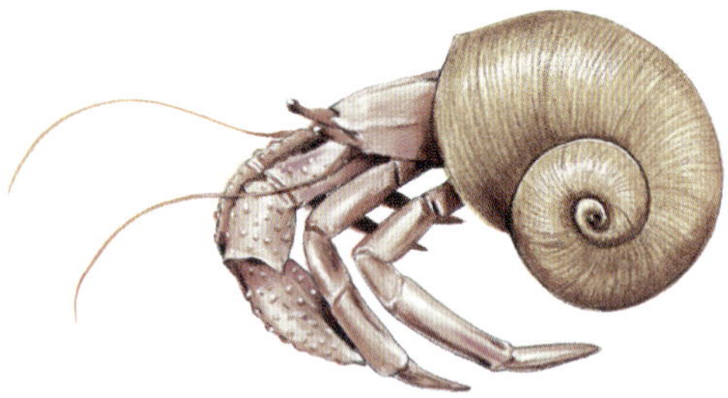

HERMIT CRAB

ARCTIC LOON

P	G	T	S	E	A	L	I	O	N
Z	G	E	K	N	R	I	U	D	Y
S	S	T	N	R	C	Y	N	X	Q
H	E	R	M	I	T	C	R	A	B
A	A	A	M	J	I	Y	C	O	D
R	S	W	L	O	C	G	Q	X	S
Q	T	X	I	Q	L	C	P	Y	L
R	A	X	A	I	O	S	P	Y	V
U	R	L	P	F	O	Z	N	E	J
G	G	B	A	R	N	A	C	L	E

SEA STAR

SEA LION

SEAL

BARNACLE

answers

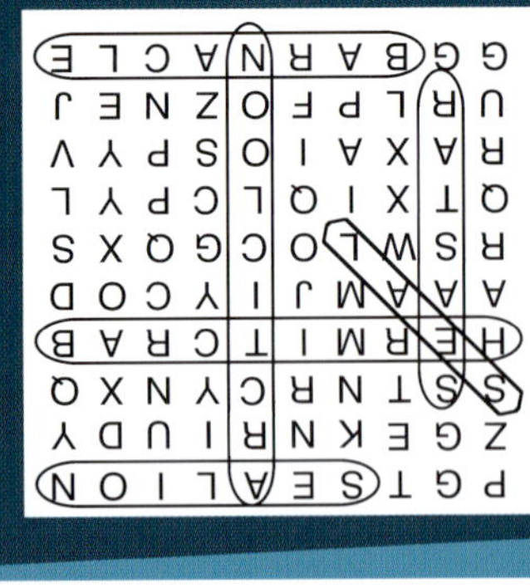

COLOR ME

Harlequin Duck

color key

CONNECT THE DOTS

These furry little rodents remain active throughout the winter beneath the snow and are a favorite food of snowy owls and foxes.

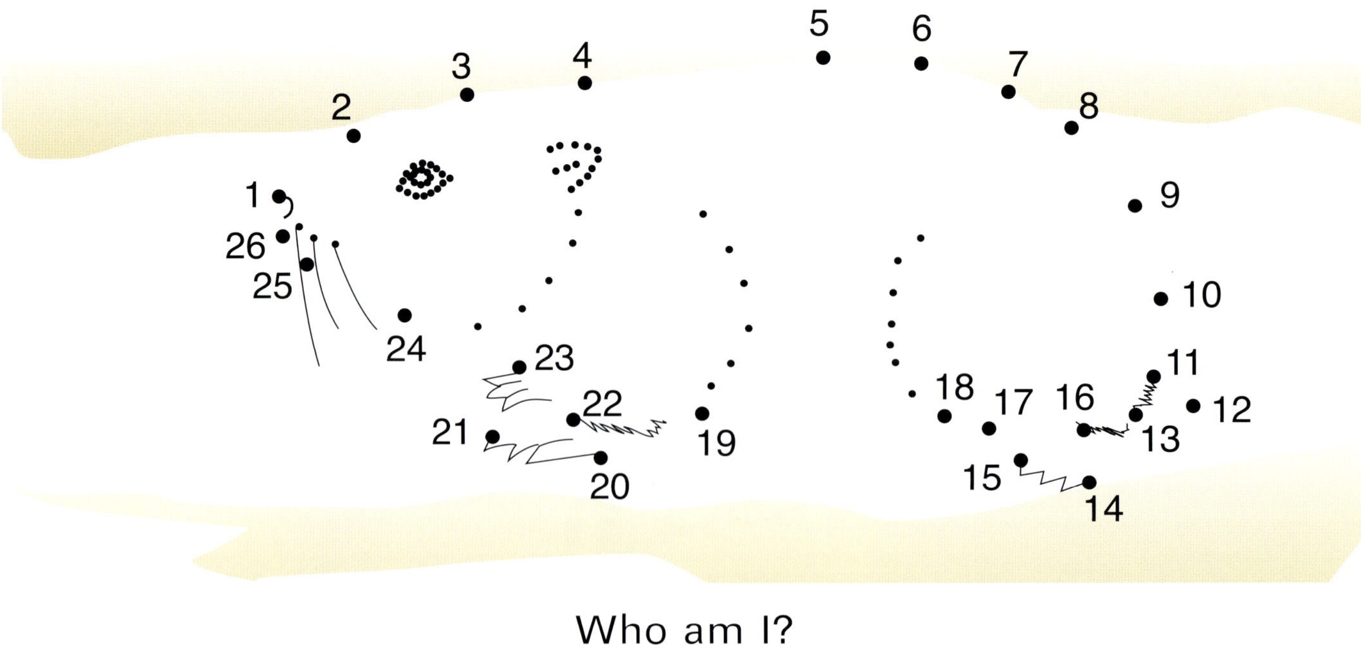

Who am I?

answer Lemming

Maze

Help the polar bear find its cubs.

Name Scramble

Unscramble the names
of these Arctic animals.

1.

o m o e s

2.

a c b r

3.

o l f w

4.

l w a e h

answers

1. Moose
2. Crab
3. Wolf
4. Whale

ODDBALL OUT

In each row, circle the seashore creature which is different from the others.

1.

1A

1B

1C

Two of these are squirrels, one is not.

2.

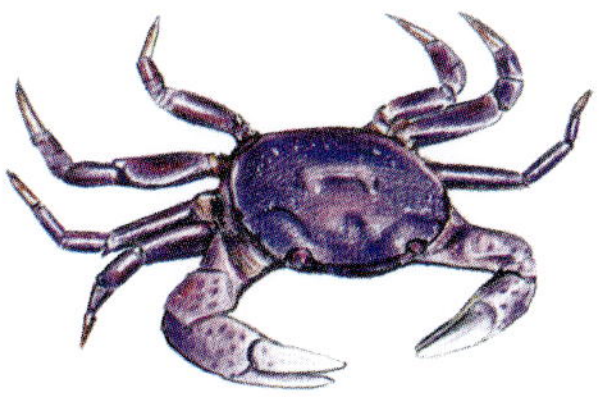

2A

2B

2C

Two of these are crabs, one is not.

3.

3A

3B

3C

Two of these are birds, one is not.

answers

1. 1C is a bird (puffin)
2. 2B is a sea star
3. 3B is a mammal (bat)

FOOD CHAIN

Draw a line between the species and its place in the food chain.

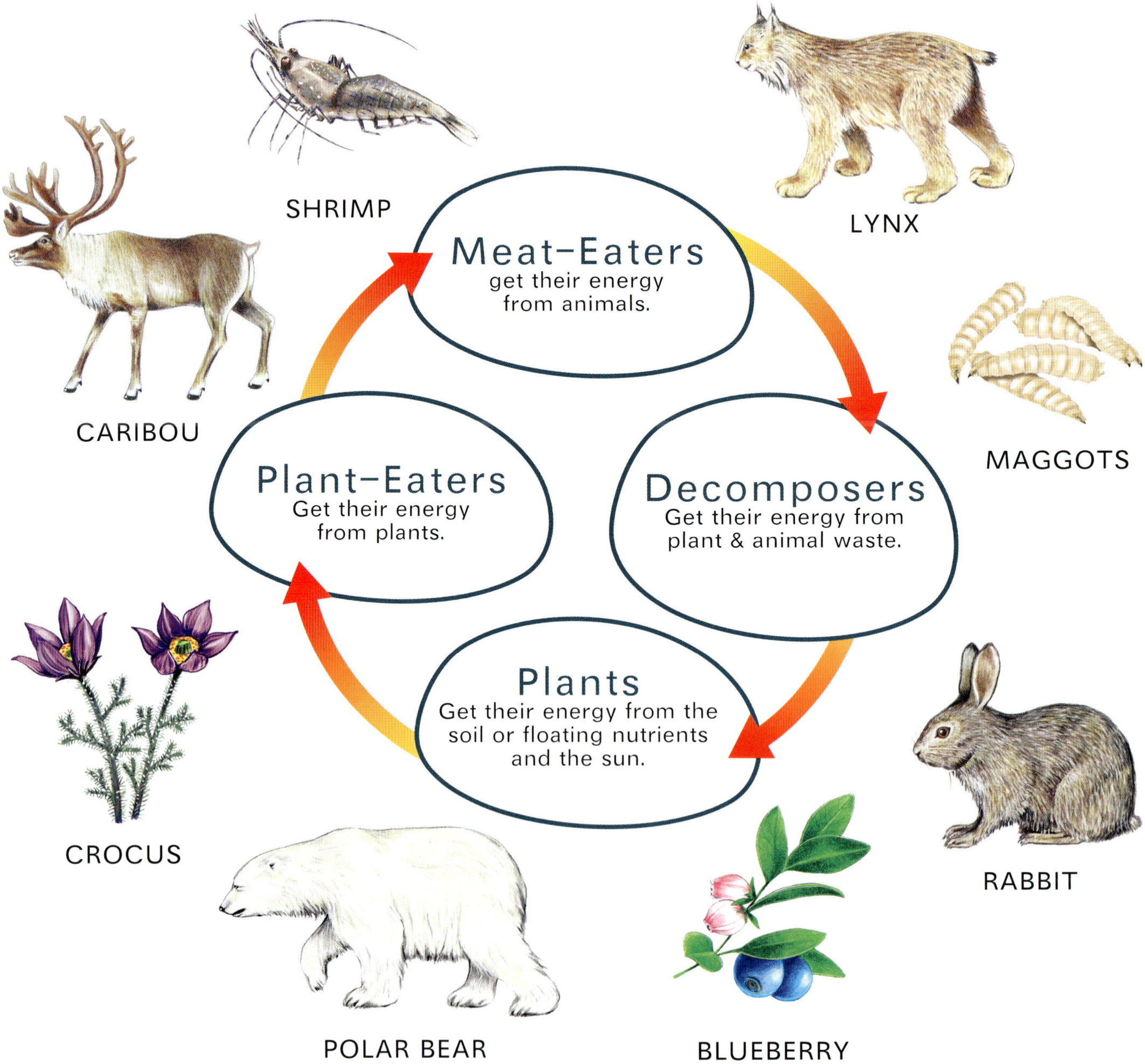

answers

Plants: Crocus, blueberry
Decomposers: Maggots, shrimp
Meat-eaters: Polar bear, lynx
Plant-eaters: Caribou, rabbit

WHO AM I?

Draw a line between the Arctic animal and its name.

1. 

2. 

3. 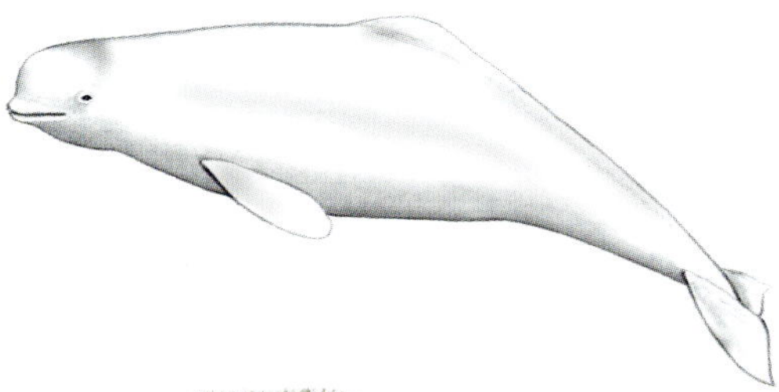

4. 

Mink

Musk Ox

Beluga

Lemming

answers

1. Lemming
2. Mink
3. Beluga
4. Musk Ox

WORD SEARCH

Arctic Fishes

P	C	C	A	O	W	G	V	Y	E
N	D	H	R	M	H	R	W	C	T
Q	E	U	C	N	I	A	Q	M	U
I	P	M	T	S	T	Y	G	N	Q
P	Q	S	I	K	E	L	P	G	P
B	L	A	C	K	F	I	S	H	G
X	O	L	C	Y	I	N	T	N	E
Q	Q	M	H	B	S	G	U	W	G
P	M	O	A	U	H	C	G	B	P
B	J	N	R	V	X	Y	P	S	J

GRAYLING

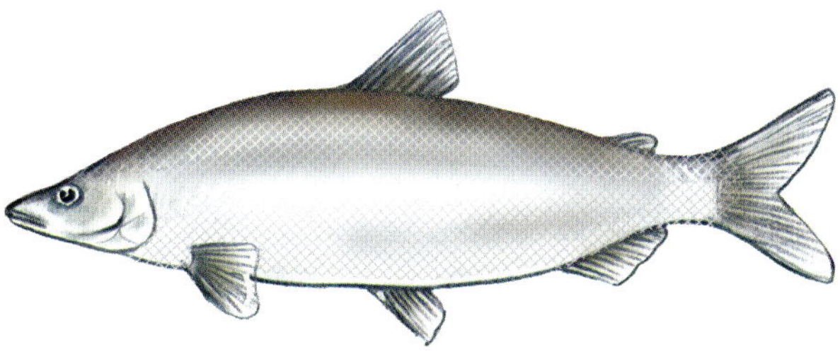

WHITEFISH

BLACKFISH

ARCTIC CHAR

CHUM SALMON

answers

SHADOW KNOW-HOW

Can you identify these Arctic animals?

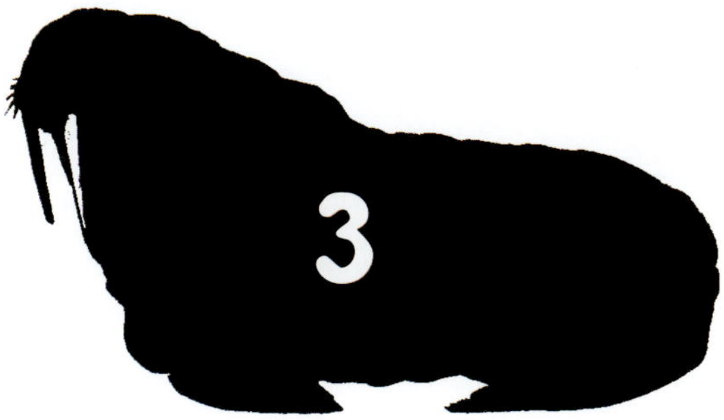

answers

1. Sea Otter
2. Polar bear
3. Walrus
4. Fish (halibut)
5. Caribou

SPOT THE DIFFERENCES

Can you spot five differences between the caribou pictures?

answers

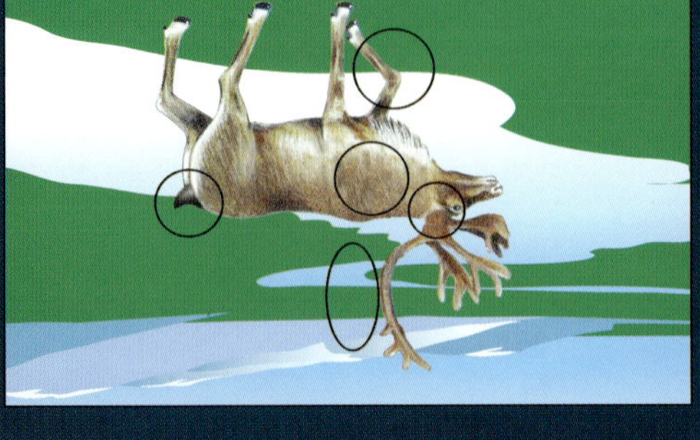

COLOR ME

Puffin

color key

CONNECT THE DOTS

I am a large, white bird that is common in Arctic regions around the world.

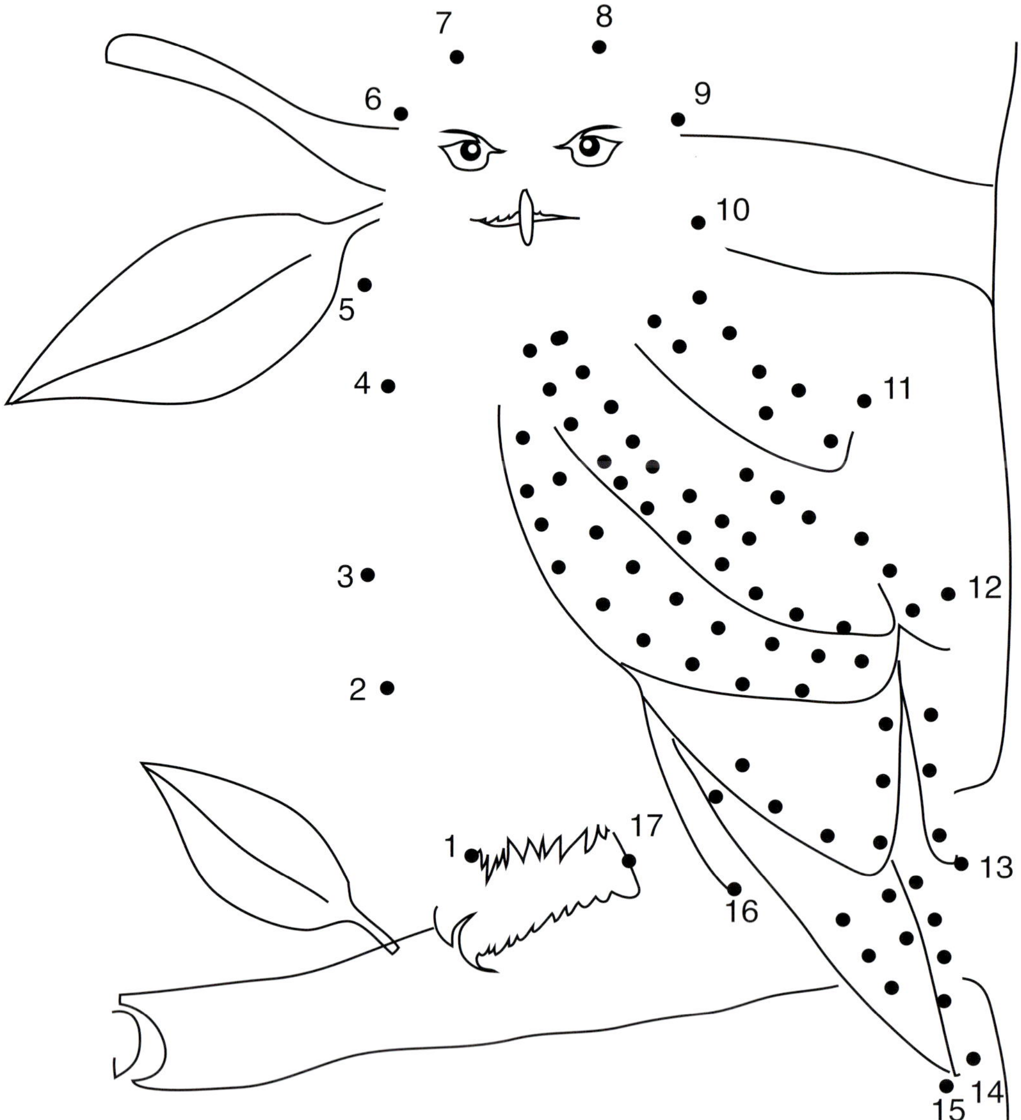

Who am I?

answer Snowy Owl

MAKE WORDS

The **bowhead whale** is a huge animal that feeds mostly on tiny shrimp (krill) it strains from the water.

How many words can you make from the letters in its name?

______________________	______________________
______________________	______________________
______________________	______________________
______________________	______________________
______________________	______________________

answers

Possible answers include: Ahead, ale, bad, bale, bead, bed, bleed, bowl, dew, dole, dow, dowel, had, haw, head, heal, heed, heel, held, hew, hold, how, howl, lead, load, owl, wale, weal, wed, wee, weed, weld, who, whoa, wow

Be an Artist

Draw this poplar bear by copying it one square at a time.

CLASS ACT

Draw a line between the animal and the group it belongs to.

SEA TURTLE

Mammals

WALRUS

BALD EAGLE

Birds

BAT

Reptiles

HALIBUT

Amphibians

RAVEN

MOUSE

Fishes

FROG

answers

Mammals - Mouse, walrus, bat
Birds - Bald eagle, raven
Reptiles - Sea turtle
Amphibians - Frog
Fishes - Halibut

WORD SEARCH

Arctic Birds

JAEGER

H	E	D	C	P	W	E	Z	E	J
I	P	I	K	A	U	A	G	P	U
D	T	A	D	E	P	F	J	Y	Y
J	A	E	G	E	R	R	F	Q	V
S	R	S	D	E	R	W	M	I	K
H	M	F	A	A	Y	L	W	Y	N
I	I	S	P	Y	M	L	A	O	W
D	G	Q	M	Q	G	V	O	C	T
I	A	I	B	M	J	F	P	Y	N
S	N	O	W	Y	O	W	L	D	H

PTARMIGAN

EIDER

PUFFIN

SNOWY OWL

answer

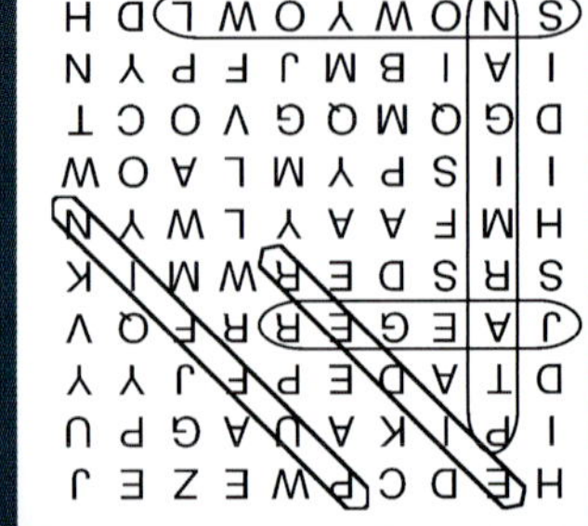

HOME SWEET HOME

Animals live where they can find food and a place to rest. Draw a line between the animal and its habitat

1. 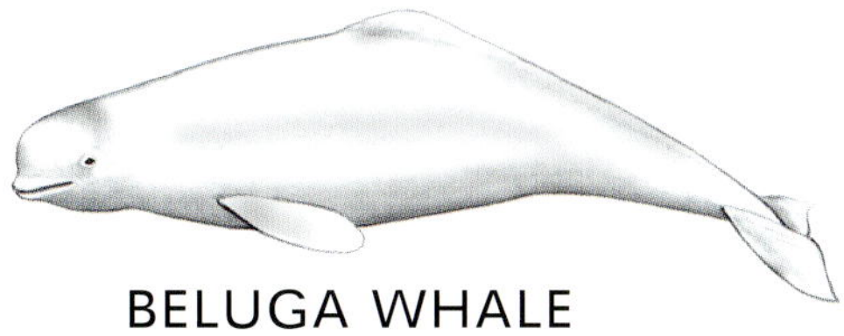

BELUGA WHALE

2. 

RIVER OTTER

3. 

HORNED PUFFIN

4. 

DALL SHEEP

(a) 

A small stream is the best place for this river mammal to hunt.

(b) 

A rocky cliff near water is the perfect place for this animal to feed and breed.

(c) 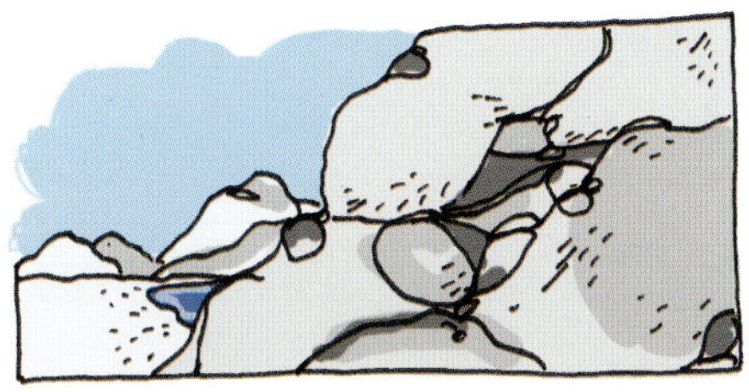

A rocky cliff is home to this agile, hoofed mammal.

(d) 

A big, wide ocean is a wonderful home for this big, wide animal.

answers

1. (d) 2. (a) 3. (b) 4. (c)

COLOR ME

Caribou

color key

Maze

A seal's favorite food is fish.
Help this seal find its meal.

Name Scramble

Unscramble the names
of these Arctic mammals.

1.

c u k d

2.

t o e r t

3.

g a e l e

4.

l s e a

answers

1. Duck
2. Otter
3. Eagle
4. Seal

ODDBALL OUT

In each row, circle the animal which is different from the others.

1. 

1A

1B

1C

Two of these are fish, one is not.

2. 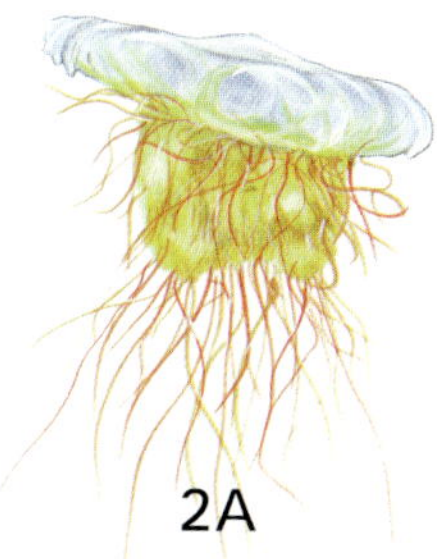

2A

2B

2C

Two of these are jellyfish, one is not.

3. 

3A

3B

3C

Two of these are plant-eaters (herbivores), one is not.

answers

1. 1B is a toad
2. 2B is a crab
3. 3A is a meat-eater (carnivore)

WORD SEARCH

Arctic Marine Mammals

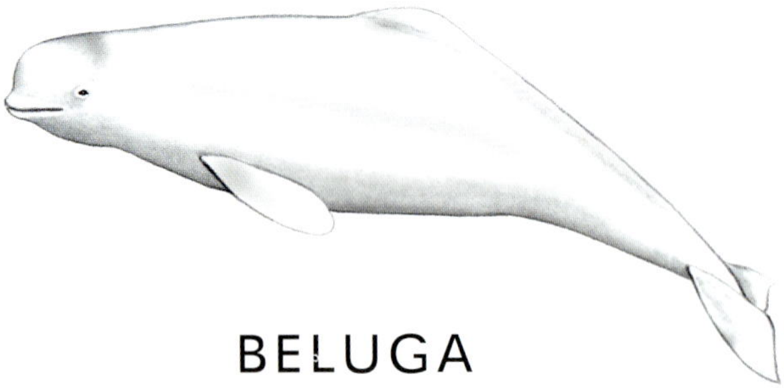

BELUGA

WALRUS

K	C	Y	S	W	A	L	R	U	S
M	G	J	Q	U	H	J	Z	Z	M
D	D	R	F	H	V	C	T	E	P
L	C	D	A	P	H	E	H	C	O
R	T	O	B	Y	Y	G	J	B	R
C	P	L	E	E	W	C	G	R	P
J	F	P	L	V	L	H	L	N	O
G	Y	H	X	K	T	U	A	F	I
R	L	I	Q	V	V	V	G	L	S
Y	T	N	V	R	I	T	F	A	E

PORPOISE

GRAY WHALE

DOLPHIN